My Caribbean Home

by

Nathan Moore

Copyright © 2012

All rights reserved.

No part of this book may be reproduced, stored in a retrieval system, or transmitted in any form, by any means without prior written permission of the publisher.

Nathan Moore

5668 Macedin Dr.

Douglasville, GA 30135

ISBN: 978-0-615-56923-9

Manufactured in the United States of America.

Contents

She Sings	1
Mother Love	4
She Observed Ceremony	6
On Walking	7
Auntie	10
Uncle	12
Seeing and Believing	14
Portrait	15
Brother Brown	16
Sweet Williams	18
Sister Rose	19
The Crossing	21
Ave Atque Vale	23
Pah C. Veerance	26
At Sea	27

Sunrise	28
Woodland Memories	29
Tropic Joys	31
Cocrico	32
That Is Love	34
Morning	36
Home	38
Memories	40
Morning	43
Kite Flying	44

Dedicated to the memory of my mother, Eugenie Moore.

-NM

She Sings

The earth is tinder dry; food, hard to find;
We travel long distances for potable water,
And at family worship we pray for rain.
She sings, "There shall be showers of blessings;
Send them upon us, O Lord.
Grant to us now a refreshing;
Come and now honor Thy word."

The smell of burning fat
Hangs heavy in the air;
It's time to smooth the wrinkles
From clothes we wear to church;
It's Thursday, and the tremor in her voice
Betrays that all's not well,
Tears course down her cheeks
But still she sings, "Fade, fade each earthly joy;
Jesus is mine. Break every tender tie;
Jesus is mine. Dark is the wilderness,
Earth has no resting place.
Jesus alone can bless; Jesus is mine."

Among her zinnias, portulaca, and fragrant herbs
Boasting yellow, red, white, and purple,
She ties, tucks, and prunes, singing
"We should be like gardens, Bright and sweet
With flow'rs, Bless'd with heaven's sunshine,
Cheer'd by gentle show'rs.
Violets are the kind words, Roses deeds of love,
Fragrant pinks and pansies, Tho'ts of God above.
Beautiful flowers, bright with morning dew;
Beautiful flow'rs, we would be like you."

Hemmed in by the waters 'round both our isles
She would sing with gusto,
"From Greenland's icy mountains,
From India's coral strands, . . .
From many an ancient river,
From many a palmy plain
They call us to deliver
Their land from error's chain."

And in her quiet moments, as her painful fingers
Expertly twitch the crochet needle
To make another table cloth or doily,
You may hear, "How tedious and tasteless the hours
When Jesus no longer I see!
Sweet prospects, sweet birds, and sweet flowers
Have lost all their sweetness to me.
The midsummer sun shines but dim;
The fields strive in vain to be gay;
But when I am happy with Him,
December's as pleasant as May."

And while one child prepares the herbs and greens for supper,
And another, the dishes, she kneads the dough
And sings, "Work for the night is coming,
When man's work is done."
Or maybe another of her favorites,
"Lord, for tomorrow and its need I do not pray;
Keep me, my God, from stain of sin, just for today.
Let me no wrong or idle word unthinking say;
Set Thou a seal upon my lips, just for today."

Through clouds and sunshine of the soul, she sang;
Day after day and hour after hour,
The hymns were for her a sustaining grace.
Now, she is gone, and has been gone
These many years, but still she sings on,
For it echoes in my heart's core.

Mother Love

How precious is your name on my lips!
Your memory refreshes as a gentle rain
As raindrops
Your counsel nurtured one you chastened

The wayward child wandered,
        stumbled
             fell

Fallen, he wallowed
    befouling himself
until
you grasped his outstretched arm
   drew him to your bosom
        wept
Weeping,
   you thrashed him clean

Cleansed
    love-imprinted
        he grew tall

Yesterday it seems
    his head fitted between your knees
        you played a tattoo on his behind
But tears
    those tears
etched themselves
        on memory's plates
Still
    now three-score years
and more
    they still avow
"I love you, son."

Your memory refreshes as a gentle rain.

She Observed Ceremony

Mangoes—She chose them
As priests select sacrificial lambs—
meticulously
No bruises, if picked up
Best plucked at first hint of ripeness
Sequester in darkness
to grow ambrosial, mouth-watering
Like incense
aroma announces readiness

Most eat mangoes randomly
She observed ceremony

After meals
by the bucketful
ritually she sat
knife in hand
mangoes on the right
pail of fresh water to the fore
At left
refuse bucket

For half-an- hour
the mango devotee
washed, sliced, and sucked
moving in smooth succession
from right to left
she was all mangoes
In the end you'd think
massacre—
a mass of skins and seeds
and yellow water lay by

So it went
all season long

 Celebrant no more
she rests
On my visits
we meet
under a spreading mango tree.

On Walking

I went walking this afternoon but paid little attention to some things that ordinarily provoke reflection. Though demanding, eventful, and significant, today's walk lacked symbolic power. It was exercise. I enjoy walking, especially outdoors, for I then do much valuable thinking and planning that grow into writing or put some fierce creatures in chains. My walking is serious business at times.

What if this afternoon I followed in my father's steps? I would have been doing more than moving my feet. When I walk in his steps, no one observing me would imagine the gravity of my behavior. In truth, for me such walking connotes profound spiritual significance and influence, especially for my children-- or my companions. Saying, "I'm walking in Father's steps" is making a confession of which many a parent would perhaps be proud. Going in his steps, I am doing business of more than earthly import. That is serious walking.

Walking in Mother's steps, however, is quite a different thing. It is stepping into sunshine from the dark shadows. The awesome spiritual power is still there, but it is wearing a lovely bright suit of light clothing in place of Dad's heavy armor. It is being a delightful inspiration, a guide who provides someone with special gifts that will forever empower him--or her--to be positively special. Walking in her steps is more a matter of being than of doing.

When my walking concerns primarily going places, though, the activity is often costly, yet not at all as affective as some other types of walking. Frequently, it is merely something geographical, going where someone else has gone, like walking the streets of

Bethsaida following in St. Peter's steps. Occasionally, such walking may carry symbolic weight, but chiefly for the walker only. Perhaps the burden then is essentially historical: I am walking where the great fisherman walked long ago.

The most significant walking often involves no paces, no steps, just doing or being. Walking can be complicated business.

Auntie

In her day she had a way
With a Singer Sewing Machine.
From Campbleton and Belleair
Young women came from far and near,
Hale and hearty or match-stick lean,
Apprenticed to Auntie with the machine.

Known for top quality work and good fit
She was tough as nails, loathe to quit,
A no-nonsense lady, at times a tad mean
When busy with work at her sewing machine.

Apprentices paid zero to learn to sew,
But that was never a matter for anxiety or chatter
Once they fetched water or kept the house clean
For the thrill to be seen working, sewing at that machine.

She cut, sewed, and fitted without benefit of pattern—
That was Aunt Neville, with flounce and frill at the side of the hill.

Learn these skills and be mistress of your scene,
Sewing with needle and thimble, not a machine.

Do what you will, but learn a skill;
Work with might and main, and use your brain.
Whether bitter like gall or mean with spleen,
Like Auntie take charge, be keen, and be master of
your machine.

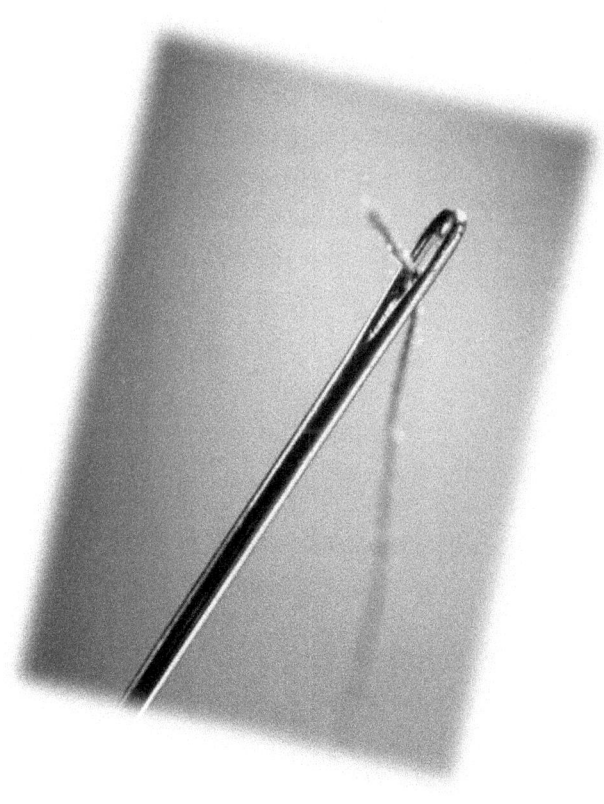

Uncle

I look backward, and what is my reward?
Memory of a painful truth
flowing from reminiscences of my youth.

My uncle, Dad's brother, earned my respect.
He was a man of parts but not an architect.
Of builders, he was easily the best in town;
no hurricane blew his structures down.

For talking, he would take the prize.
A man of many words, wise in our eyes.
But came a day when all would say,
"He was from a strange mold;
All that glistens is not gold."

O how I wish I could forget!
The day of our betrayal rankles in my memory yet.
My uncle was a coward and a thief!
Nothing he has done since shakes that belief.

The story is painful but quickly told—
he raped Dad's field of its black gold.

Father tended the family's plot--
acres of cocoa, bananas, cassava, what not.
If good for food, 'twas there,
objects of Dad's tender care.

We children toiled too, come sun or rain,
delighting in mango, sapodilla, sugar-cane.
But cocoa was the chief focus of our attention—
the money crop, cocoa had no rival in that function.

That year the trees were laden from ground to top,
assurance of a bountiful golden crop.
Daily Dad monitored the yellowing field.
Eyes gleaming, he envisioned extraordinary yield,

"Come Monday, lads, you'll go with me
to reap ripe pods from every tree."
Boots, bags, knives and rods—
on Monday we were all ready to pluck the pods.

Having gone to the field, none could believe what we found—
heaps and heaps of empty pods lying all around.
While our family knelt in church to pray,
Uncle and his brood reaped the field and took the crop away.

Neighbors commiserate, heave many a sigh.
As for me, I never again could look my uncle in the eye.

Many years have come and gone
but the memories linger and prick as a thorn.
When we talk of Uncle, no one shakes my belief—
Uncle, my uncle, remains a coward and a thief.

Seeing and Believing

I saw James pluck bird peppers
from the tree, toss them in his mouth,
gulp, blink his eyes, swallow,
and I saw the peppers no more.

Some say seeing is believing,
but I'm no believer.
Perhaps not a seer either.
Those impossibly hot peppers
disappeared in James' mouth.

But tasting bird peppers once,
I dare not affirm James ate them.
He seemed too composed
too much at ease that hot day.

I saw no reddening of his eyes,
no burst of beads of sweat
from face—or anywhere else.

He called for no water,
no food, no antidote—nothing.
Must I doubt my seeing, or the saying?
Perhaps this is a matter of definition.

Peppers disappeared in James' mouth—
chewed, gulped, ingested, taken in.
Ah! taken in. That's a new twist.
Were those peppers or was I taken in?
I shall never know for James will never tell.

A Portrait

If a tree, he would be a poui
that you find on the forest floor,
mature, weathered—hard,
ideal for enduring service,
even if cross-grained at times
and not particularly handsome.

Some may flinch at his hardness,
but observed carefully, he exudes a rugged
charm, especially when his fleeting smile
betrays perfect, glistening white teeth.

I think of him as the family sphinx.
Ask him a question
but expect no easy response,
rather, something riddle-like,
demanding keen thought and
careful reflection. Exasperating, some think.
Noah they call him; I call him Builder.

His prize-winning sailboats moulder
among weeds on Tobago's shores
while he labors to build another,
a replica, perhaps, of the Platonic ideal.
That's my brother. Yes, he is a poui.

Brother Brown

You were the sweet singer of our congregation
with a voice inimitable, unique
that conveyed joy and peace
I still remember that Christmas morn
you roused us from slumber singing,
"There's a stranger at your door
Let Him in."

Dear Brother Brown,
teller of tall hunting tales
that scared us out of our wits
in our sleep we saw the demons
at the base of the silk cotton tree
heard them howl at the blast
of your gunpowder charge
and wondered at your adventures
with those devilish lights that led
hunters among thorn bushes and nettles

You taught us to fish with harpoons
and made our eyes pop at fish you caught
so large that you had to drag them home
You were the workman all longed for
because you never stinted on time
nor fudged on excellence of quality
You are the worker the angel
stooped to honor with a crown
that you did not receive because
you never raised your head from your
labor that the coronet should slip into place

Many declared that you were poor
but few were blessed with your riches
You brought such joy to our home
that we children yearned for your visits
The morning you killed the snake
on the avocado tree with one blast
from grandpa's rusty shotgun
you were our hero and magician

Singer, preacher, father, worker, Christian—
You gave distinction to each role
Brother Brown
Man of parts
A living legend
How we all loved and treasured you!
We wanted to keep you among us
forever
You should have walked that day
but you rode the bus to town
and never got back home

because the bus ran off the road
Into the woods and took you with it
You could not walk away
Your people laid you tenderly to rest
to await the trumpet call
Sweet be your rest, Brother Brown.

Sweet Williams

You never found an axe too heavy for you to wield
no tree you could not fell single-handedly
no man who could exhaust you in the sawpit
Sweet Williams, every tree learns to respect the wind.
The one that stands up to it
surely breaks at last.
Learn a lesson from one who has yet to lose a bet
from one who has humbled the best among men.

You may be right, sir
but everyone in this village knows
better than to stand up
to Williams, the rock of Gibraltar
Nothing,
not rain or hurricane
keeps him from going where he wishes.
That's not a boast, sir;
it is a fact of life.

Early one morning
alone,
Williams axed a six-foot cypress tree—
Diameter, not height--
it tumbled
but not alone
Williams sprawled strangely
far from the stump
his chest like pulp—
struck by the grim reaper.

Sister Rose

We called her Sister Rose
not because she was a beauty to behold
but that she was a joy to associate with
exuding assurance, positiveness;
yet most of us never saw her stand.
She was always lying in bed
paralyzed;

only her fingers moved
but she sang like a songbird
powerful and delightful to hear
a powerhouse she was
and sage

Mothers yearned to have their girls taught by her.
They too became songbirds
Young men felt proud to serve her
proud to be in the carrying team of four;
to fathers, she was the village saint
counselor and peacemaker—
Sister Rose

One day she was called away
to rest
We bore her to her resting place
We wept
and sang joyful songs
of a golden morning
feeling sure that she would rise

would bloom again
sing angel-like
and walk—
Sister Rose.

The Crossing

Bobby never heard of Charon,
but he was the ferryman one day
and never would forget it.

Every villager knew the treacherous
passage at Big Rock, the shortest course
between two villages across the bay
where at times the current was strong
the waves devilish and the reef sinister.
Experienced boatmen approach the passage
with respect and dread; others, at their peril.

The waves surged high that morning
but the narrow passage seemed inviting in calm
moments
Two men confidently plied their oars
in a small boat heading for Charlotteville
Two women and a child sat quiet toward the stern.

Near the passage the oarsmen paused
awaiting the safe moment.
Then with swift sure strokes,
they dashed to cross the narrow opening,
but suddenly a devilish wave roared high and fast
and swept the boat broadside toward the reef.

Caught in the shallows
the craft grated and spilled its burden on the rocks.

Heroically both men fought the waves
to save their charges
caught and struggled in the foam
to get them to the craft.
The women in panic fought to save the child
They were all losers.
Battered, bruised, and bleeding
the boatmen bore three bodies to the shore.

If you have seen a man crawl
hold his belly and bawl
you've seen a man who knows sorrow.

Ave Atque Vale

Charlotteville,
dearest village of the isle—
seen from the hills,
how colorful, how fair—
from Campbleton
to Top River and Belleair.

In November,
you plaster your green hillsides
yellow and scarlet
with poui blossoms
and stately immortelles,
complementing a veritable
Joseph's coat of colors
from houses hugging the hills.

Alas, memories all
of days that are no more.
Eden had its serpent,
and you, the hurricanes—
a devil's baneful breath.

Gone are the cocoa crops that kept whole families at work,
gone, too, thriving fields, flourishing
gardens of bananas,
plantains, potatoes, tannias, dasheen
yams and sugar cane.

And where's the sawpit?
where, the sinewy arms,
masters of the whipsaw and the axe?
Memories all,
kept alive by faithful re-enactments—
blessed heritage.

Recall, fortunate few, the Easter festivities:
from Long Rock boat races back to bay—
see the ropy rippling muscles
that ply the oars,
bows cutting white ribbons,
sterns whisking white wakes.

Your sons once climbed the greasy pole:
sturdy bamboo firmly planted
in the sand and generously greased white
from base to top,
crowned with choice prizes
for the valiant climber.

Today your fishermen—
fond farewell to sails and oars—
ply the deeps
propelled by Yamahas, Evinrudes, and Johnsons,
often, like their forebears, returning
flush with fish
enough for villagers—and more.
They daily ply a lively trade.

Today the world paints you fishing paradise
par excellence,

and faring from far
they come, your children and visitors
lured by the beauties of the undersea
—manta rays, brain corals
and myriad denizens of the deeps.
Yearning, yearly they return
pilgrims on their sacred quest.

One glory has departed;
another has been born.
Subsistence shifts from strand to sea.
From Europe, the Americas, and beyond,
your children come and go—
leaders and survivors—
you taught them well.
Ave atque vale, Charlotteville!

Pah C. Veerance

You filthy water hole,
are you still there?
Do you still lure children,
afraid of the dark,
to fill their buckets with your scum?

Baneful deliverer,
you took advantage of our ignorance.
Yes, we knew you were not meant for human lips.
But no one thought you
a potential fountain of woe!
What mercy saved us
from a painful death those many years?

How many thrashings we endured
because someone maliciously
revealed our youthful indiscretions!
Today we tremble, distraught
at the magnitude of the evil
to which you lured us.
Alas! We never heard of *E. coli*.
But now we shudder at the thought,
suffering nightmares at the possibilities.

How shall we reward you
to amply repay our misery?
Derisive laughter is poor return
for our years of anxiety and remorse.
A name! That you shall have;
cognomen reminiscent of your bane:
Pah C. Veerance we name you,
and Pah C. Verance you shall be
as long as these lines live.

At Sea

Grimly gripping the thwarts,
I hang on for dear life
as our boat drives up each rising wave
then drops into bottomless troughs.
Drooling gall,
stomach long empty, I heave.
O for solid earth!
What am I doing here?
Dreams of fishing--
the horizon changes with each surge and fall.
Soaked and shaking with cold,
I hold on as each drenching spray sweeps past.

The helmsman sits calmly,
eyes fixed ahead on nothing but the heaving sea,
resignedly accepting each blast of spray.
Occasionally, he glances at me
and smiles.

I tighten my grip and hope.

Sunrise

O, sunrise!
  glorious!
dawn
   life
     light
 energy
      warmth
day's childhood that

 sets blood
      surging!
nature's smile

  hope to our world

fountain of joy
     moment of
        ecstasy!
ah!
  sunrise!

   my daily
      rebirth.

Woodland Memories

Sweet the music wafting on the breeze,
notes of a feathery chorister,
heart bursting with joyous melodies.

You don't know it, sweet singer, but you are
lifting spirits, rolling life's burdens away,
filling one heart with a yearning
to match you in gusto, rival you in praise.

You bring to mind moments when song
issues forth from soul fountains
like flights of monarch butterflies sailing
among flowers in the meadow.

Sing me a song of soft sunshine
smiling in the morning air
filtering through boughs, twigs, and leaves,
streaming like rays reaching from the skies to earth.

You sing as though you know what it is
to triumph over pain; tell me whence
came that song to you, what master musician
schooled you into seemingly effortless utterance
of a song at once heart-searching and refreshing?

Selfless one, at least, grant me one glimpse of yourself,
assurance that you are a messenger of peace,
no woodland sprite.

Long shall your song echo in my soul.

Tropic Joys

Thanks for things that bring me joy
that set me smiling like a child
rare juices from my tropic isles
green nuts and fruits ambrosial

The plain raw juice of sugar cane
julie mangoes and little paw
guavas, portugals, and French cashew
shaddocks, sapodillas, sour-sops.

The jabs and quips of calypsos
lampooning subjects high and low
lyrics well matched with tune and beat
set me humming, tapping with my feet

My wildest joy comes from the pan
played by one expert or a big band
road marches calypsos excite
the classics best take me to a high.

These cited here are just the start
of what lures me to my home isles
Flora and fauna may claim their part
demanding thanks for what brings smiles.

Cocrico

Bird of stealth, the farmer's bane,
destroyer of fruits, sprouts, and grain,
fearless interloper, noisy pheasant,
why take such pains to be unpleasant?

Time was you would be fair game
for huntsman and cooks, who claim
no chicken yields a tastier meat
as you no rooster's crow can beat.

Now, thanks to Flora, you're protected,
untouchable as if infected,
unless you remove the charm
by depredations on someone's farm.

Mangoes, guava, and pigeon peas,
corn in the ground, plums on the trees,
nothing is safe from your visitation
unless one reaps it in anticipation.

Some birds sing songs that bring us pleasure;
you make noises, but their rhythms we treasure.
Could you not choose a better hour
your raucous noises on us to shower?

You have a secret. Would you please tell,
unless it's a matter best left, well,
alone: Why choose Tobago for your home
and never to the sister isle you deign to roam?

For that choice alone we hold you dear
and will pretend for you we'll ever care;
so Trinidadians will always yearn to know
what's special about a cocrico.

That Is Love

He heard a cry of anguish
the scream of a mother
discovering the lifeless form of her infant
she left gurgling in its cradle
He knew that gut wrenching wail
the sound of helplessness
of pain no balm can relieve
He found her crouching, fetal
whimpering
Quietly, he sat beside her
gently, ever so gently
he touched her heaving shoulders
He knew her pain.

Five years she yearned for that child
more years she envied happy mothers
burping their babies contentedly
eyes twinkling at infant smiles
Monthly the kits mocked her fruitless efforts
monthly she felt cheated by the plague
Each new birth laughed in her face
shouting barren, barren, barren
each a reminder of her curse

How many prayers
silent petitions for mercy
How many promises she made
when joyful days went bitter with stillbirths
and then came Victoria
the fulfillment of all her dreams

She lived for little Victoria
Nothing, nothing, nothing was too good for her
That baby was perfect
mother's joy
God's gift of love and beauty

And now
was it a cruel joke?

He knew her pain
and longed to bring her relief
so he sat and wept beside her

That is love, I thought.

Morning

Morning glows rosy on distant hills
  Blood surges
    urge for briskness
      walking
        chopping
          running

Sails bulge in the brisk breeze
  wakes white with frothy foam
    Engines snort in urgency
    in a frenzy
      fishermen dash
        for feeding fish

Aroma of hot coffee
    frying fish
      fresh-baked loaves
      hang in the air

Parrots
  green and gold
    wing their ways
      chattering
        to the mango trees
          fresh green fruit clatter earthward
          waste of the wild ones

Gulls laugh
  giddy with gladness
    In their feeding frenzy

Ropy muscles ripple
  as axe heads flash
    in soft sunlight
      and bite bite bite
        into wild wood

Another day is busy
  pregnant with life's variety.

Home

The stream gurgles its perpetual praise song
in concert with the frogs on the banks and
the whistling of the winds through the casuarina
above.

The blue of the skies is mirrored in the waters beneath
with splashes of white where waves lash the black rocks,
recede, and splash again in perfect rhythm.

And the November hillsides blaze with immortelles in crimson bloom
competing with the pinks and yellows of pouis
in the tropic forests of green.

The houses of the little fishing village
hug the hillsides in a patchwork of painted roofs
as from the pages of a child's coloring book.

In the waters of the bay ride a dozen fishing boats at anchor,
little brothers and sisters to the yachts of foreigners
on extended visits from distant lands.

A narrow road snakes down the hillside and along
the edge of the bay,
then, octopus-like, branches, leading into the
heart of the community.

Welcome to Charlotteville,
my childhood home.

Memories

I think of her with gratitude
and pray for her in love
because she was precious to me
even when she caused me pain

I am grateful for her when I remember
how lovingly she cared for me
even to chastising me severely
when I strayed from the path
she taught me to go

I pray for her in love
because she made mistakes
and did not know it
She loved as no one else I knew
gave willingly and deeply
until it hurt her into tears

I made her weep
but she never gave up loving me.
She was most precious to me
because she gave even if it meant
she was deprived of necessary food
and items for which she saved for years

She gave and never reminded me
of her sacrifices and suffering
From her I learned what love is
I shall never forget her singing
through her tears
her singing in anguish and misery
singing in joy
and, yes, singing in hope

She was always singing
and the songs she sang
were precious, instructive, memorable
some, songs from school days
but most, hymns of faith, hope, and courage

How can I forget a whipping
which to this day I know
I did not deserve?
But the pain of that whipping
came from seeing her cry
just as hard as I cried from my hurt

She yearned for assurance
that I would not be lost
that I would turn from waywardness
into the path of righteousness
She loved me into goodness

And now that she is at rest
many a day I catch myself
praying for her
but really praying for myself
Praying that I will live
worthy of her memory
worthy of her love
worthy of her greatest gift to me
the love of reading

Mother, blessed you are among women!

Morning

Morning creeps upon us
lighting the hills and valleys
in a soft gold that touches us with wonder.
It is a time of hope,
of soul yearning for better moments,
joyous experiences, better things.

Today is a clean slate,
an opportunity and a challenge,
not to keep it clean,
but to imprint on it what will endure
the crush of time and awful circumstance.

Would that morning last all day!
Then would hearts ever beat
 with fresh purpose and determination,
eyes twinkle with brightness and eager anticipation,
hands reach out to touch with wonder
and lift the burdens of the weak,
ears hear cries of infant innocence and chatter,
lips utter words of cheer, hope, and trust.

Mornings! precious moments of vibrancy,
visions of freshness and possibilities,
recurring pictures of our persistent dreams.
Eternal springtime of the human soul—
Morning.

Kite Flying

Soar, my white-winged bird;
head for the clouds scudding above you.
My spirit is climbing with you;
take me to the blue beyond.
I clutch this string to keep you secure
lest you slip away and leave me marooned here
while you play among the sun-bathed clouds,
leave me groveling in despair and anxiety
bowed under cares too heavy for one to bear.

The wind's our friend and foe;
too strong, you snap this string
and flutter to a watery grave;
too weak, you fall to roost in the trees,
a scarecrow, bleached by sun and rain;
just right, we climb and laugh with the hawks
playing hide and seek among the clouds.
What joy, like hawks to rise and glide
untethered to earth
free, free, free!

If only for a moment, let me ride the currents,
leaving behind life's miseries and aches.
For a moment?
No! I'd stay conjoined to earth;
she yet holds in thrall those most dear to me.
Together we will rise or stay
awaiting the moment of change.

Come back, my white-winged bird;
come back.
As earth draws me to her bosom,
so I haul you in.

I must await the precious moment.

About the Author

A true Trinibagonian (born in Mayaro, Trinidad, grew up in Charlotteville, Tobago) Nathan Moore began writing poetry after retiring from teaching English language and literature at Walla Walla College in the State of Washington and at Alabama State University in Montgomery, Alabama. He writes poems reminiscent of life in Tobago, especially of villagers whose experiences affected his developing character. The beauty of the flora and fauna of the islands figure prominently in his writing even if some aspects of those, especially immortelles, were obliterated by hurricane Flora.